# LIFE AND LOVE

The CHRISTIAN IDENTITY SERIES allows the modern layman to find meaning in the teachings of Christ, to help him anchor his personality in ageless values, to show him how christianity can be lived today. The series provides the layman with information about the human condition, the questions life raises, and the solutions that the gospel message can offer to existence. Since christian identity cannot be found in isolation, the series addresses itself to the total human community. It is designed for private reading, for classes in religious education, and for study groups. Each volume contains discussion questions, suggestions for further readings, and multi-media.

MATTHEW EUSSEN, EDITOR
*Center for Studies in Religious Education*

# LIFE AND LOVE

*By Manuel Joseph Costa & Matthew Eussen • Christian Identity Series • GEO. A. PFLAUM PUBLISHER • Dayton, Ohio 1970*

NIHIL OBSTAT
Cletus Wessels, S.T.D.
Censor Deputatus

IMPRIMATUR
✠ James J. Byrne, S.T.D.
Archbishop of Dubuque
January 27, 1970

All of the photos in this book are the
work of Paul Tucker

Selections from *The Little Prince* by Antoine De Saint-
Exupery. Copyright 1943. Used with permission of the
publisher, Harcourt, Brace & World of New York.

Library of Congress Catalogue Card Number:
79-114725

Copyright © 1970 by Manuel Joseph Costa & Matthew Eussen

Geo. A. Pflaum, Publisher
38 West Fifth Street, Dayton, Ohio 45402

Manufactured in the United States of America

# CONTENTS

## FOREWORD

Because of the strange confluences of history—the awareness of persons, the humanitarian revolutions, the discoveries of the behavioral sciences—christianity suddenly finds itself in a position to carry out in a practical way the saying, "Love your neighbor as yourself." After twenty centuries of preaching, crusades, theologizing, we are finally beginning to see what is involved in that simple statement, what love of self means and what the art of loving others demands.

In this book the authors set a christian context in which personalism is to be understood. This movement is one that we, as disciples of Christ, cannot afford to miss. The second chapter draws in detail the monological person, his patterns of behavior and attitudes toward other persons. The point of the chapter is not to find fault with others, but to understand ourselves better. Without being aware of the limits we have already set for ourselves and the possible pitfalls, it is difficult to take genuine love seriously.

The remainder of the book deals with how we can become dialogical persons. All too frequently we are tempted to say there is nothing to being aware of others. However, the authors see this as a lifelong task that must be worked out—and worked at.

This book, then, is about the most basic elements of the christian's vocation. It treats of himself, his identity and his attitude. In the Epilogue a few practical techniques are offered which the reader may want to use to become a dialogical person, a more effective christian, and to help others do the same.

MATTHEW EUSSEN

# One

# PEOPLE NEED PEOPLE

We live in the age of personalism. Today, mankind is growing out of its self-centered childhood and is struggling to find itself. Out of the growing pains emerges the discovery that persons are free to give themselves to others; that they are and should be self-giving.

Childhood's selfish actions are scolded by psychologists, sociologists, philosophers, theologians, folksingers, poets and novelists. The defenses built up against the new-found altruism are dynamited by flower-power, love-power and atomic power. Mankind's adolescent aggressiveness directs itself against the so-called establishment which is thought to hamper the creativity of youth. Consequently, re-

bellion and revolution are born, forces that will not be stilled.

Uncontrolled aggression has been met with clubs and dogs. The enthusiasm of youth, however, is not squelched so easily. Brutality cannot disguise and obscure the search for values. No matter how turbulent that search, it is conducted in honesty and sincerity. The goal is the brotherhood of man, relief for the poor, and harmony for nations.

To grow into adulthood, mankind is torn from the security of its childhood and must be willing to risk the challenge of the unknown. Fulfillment does not come from self-aggrandizement, but from giving to others. Whenever the foundations of life are ripped up, security is destroyed, because becoming an adult means offering one's destiny and future freely to others. Involvement with other persons is a frightening endeavor. Self-revelation can be a painful and unpredictable experience. Therefore each man risks his own future when he attempts to give himself in concern for another. But once on the path, turning back is even more difficult.

Although the sudden realization that the needs of people and the destiny of persons are more important than a production schedule or a traveler's timetable, the movement is as old as mankind. The evolution of this movement has been difficult. And its development must emerge further before it can be brought to fulfillment.

The movement was given a special impetus by Christ. Although the commandment to love one's neighbor as self had been given to the Hebrew nomads centuries before, it was repeated by the human voice of God to a few followers. As these disciples followed the Roman trade routes, the message of love announced became a threat to the Roman establishment. In spite of the many accusations the Romans brought against the christians, they admired their love for one another.

Even though the courts of Rome sent many christians to their death, the movement grew. The concern of these christians was the slave, the beggar, the outcast. The checkered history of the movement has become a favorite subject of historians and novelists alike. However, its yardstick has always been growth into maturity according to the stature of Christ.

To grow according to the stature of Christ, as St. Paul says, means imitating the life of Christ. Christ's life was a life lived only for the sake of men. Between the date of his birth and the final moment of total self-giving in death on the cross, he preached the dignity of each person. He preached love of all men; he criticized the hypocrisy of the established religion and tore at the phoniness of life. He acted out of compassion, mercy and patience. He ripped away the superficialities of human existence and exposed the true meaning and value of man. His life was one of involvement and friendship with others.

"Love your neighbor as yourself" is a message that touches the center of human life. Through these few words, Christ says that true human maturity lies in concern and involvement with others.

Some think of this commandment as two separate commands: one referring to our neighbor, the other referring to our own maturity. However, this is a gross misunderstanding. What Christ is telling us is that if we love ourselves we will love our neighbor. We cannot truly love self without loving our fellowman. In other words, we cannot love ourselves without encountering the other. And conversely, without reaching out to other men, we cannot find our own fulfillment. Human maturity, fulfillment, perfection and holiness are not achieved in isolation and alienation; they are accomplished only with and through others.

In the simple statement, "Love your neighbor as yourself," Christ points out the nature of man. Human maturity is essentially self-giving. Psychologists are beginning to discover the significance of calling man a social animal. His orientation ought to be to his fellowman. To the extent that he lives for others he is completely human. To the extent that he cuts himself off from such relationships, he is failing his humanity.

A man who truly loves no longer fears others. They stop being a threat to his security. He is no longer at war with himself and the world as he tries to make something of his life. He has found the

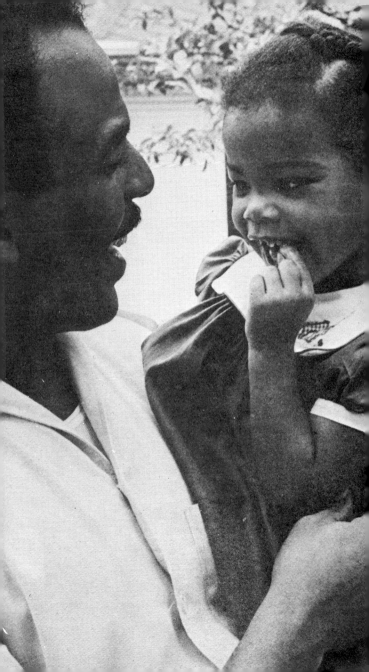

perfection he is looking for in love. He need not look further.

Childhood is left behind. The consciousness of the mature man has expanded to include others. He no longer sees himself as the center of a world in which others exist only for his pleasure. The other as a person is now very much his interest. He is aware of his duties and obligations to his neighbor. Through love he moves beyond justice. The "me" for whose service the total environment existed has disappeared. In childhood, whatever afforded me pleasure was to be admitted into my circle of consciousness and existence. Whatever impeded my complete gratification was resisted. The world existed only for me and what could be gained from it according to my own set of values.

The child feels secure in his own world in which he is master; strangers are a threat to that world. The child is satisfied with the status quo and resents any change in his secure world. Therefore, instead of being outgoing, he is turned in on himself. The other does not really exist for him. Consequently he cannot give himself to that other. There is no one to give himself to. All persons who enter his world are there for his welfare.

The child is self-centered; the mature man is willing to take the risks involved in being other-centered. He does not flee the unfamiliar which threatens his security. The unknown is a creative challenge. The child is self-sufficient, self-satisfied. He is interested only in himself. He has not learned to appreciate the other person and therefore has no reason to leave his walled city.

The man who follows the command of Christ to love his neighbor as himself has left the world of childhood behind. He has found a world beyond himself, a world more important than himself, the world of the other. And in this world he exercises his talents.

The mature christian, that is, the mature man, has also left behind the aggressiveness of youth. The will to power does not dominate his life. He does not have to conquer others to feel wanted, needed. He does not have to prove himself. Failure in the competition of daily life does not matter because full humanity is more important to him. Social pressures do not matter because love motivates him.

Maturity and self-fulfillment can be found only in encounter with others. We feel a great need to fight alienation, to struggle against loneliness. We want to belong to someone, to share our lives. In spite of this urge and need, we do not know how our lives can become a part of someone else. Nevertheless we search in the hope of being able to discover the true meaning of encounter. Life cannot be lived alone. The challenge of human life is to find ourselves through others.

A man's value is measured especially by his ability to make genuine contacts with others. Yet so many fail to find genuine friendship, an authentic involvement. The glad-handers and the back-slappers seem to move easily in society, yet often they are locked in loneliness. Because someone has drinking buddies and business associates, he may be under the illusion that he has many friends. The clown in the group has illusions of popularity, but he is alone. As long as a person is useful, he is in great demand. Others seem to reach out to him, but often it is only to use him for their own purposes.

All of us need other people in our lives, and many will go to any lengths to quiet this need. To find authentic encounter, we must share ourselves as we really are and allow others into our lives.

Although we may realize the need for people in our lives, frequently we fail to open ourselves to another. The tempo of modern life interrupts the time needed to encounter another. There is a job to be done, an appointment to be kept, a bus to catch. Any number of excuses keep us from seeing the other person as he is.

Time is perhaps the most basic element necessary to realize involvement with another and also the one least available. Also, "I have no time" is most often used to excuse and to escape involvement. To allow another to enter our life and to share it with him, we must learn to give of our own time generously. We must allow life to slow down so that persons can become more important than the hands on the clock or the mechanism within.

But just gaining minutes is not enough. Unless the minutes gained can be profitably spent to become genuinely interested in another, life will be lonely and futile. Genuine interest means to be interested in someone's hobby, his work, his homelife, his dreams, his likes, his dislikes, his feelings. This kind of sharing with another person leads to knowledge and love.

Given the time and the genuine desire to know another, we also need the courage to take the risk. To share oneself with another and open one's life involves the risk of being hurt. The knowledge another has gives him power over us. Although we extend a gesture of friendship, it may not be accepted. Although we may welcome another into our life, the other may not have room for us. Such a rejection can be discouraging, causing us to question our own self-worth.

Perhaps the immediate reaction to rejection is to withdraw from any involvement, but this cuts ourselves off from maturity. Discouragement is unnecessary if our openness has been genuine. We have given ourselves unreservedly and offered someone an opportunity that he did not recognize or chose not to accept.

The proof of our genuineness is whether or not we allow the other the freedom to reject us. Do we give him that right? Do we allow him to turn away without our becoming embittered, sarcastic, jealous, tactless? This is really the ultimate test of self-giving—to allow the other to accept or to reject. This is the giving of self without expecting anything in return. This is human generosity.

All of us have a great need to share our thoughts, to be understood, to be encouraged, to be helped. Once we have been accepted, however, do we press ourselves on the other so that we do not hear his need? Concentration on ourselves hinders relationships. To be involved with someone there must be a corresponding *un*-involvement with self. We must listen to the other. The ability to listen to another is a rare gift that is not readily found. An attitude of listening means forgetting self-sufficiency long enough to hear the other.

In listening we meet the paradox of human growth and development. While we allow someone else to absorb our attention, while we give ourselves over to him, we grow and find ourselves. The more we are able to give ourselves to another, the more real, the more human do we become and the more we discover ourselves.

We grow by giving and receiving within community. The human organism is born into, nourished by, participates in, and communicates with the world of persons. The individual comes to full stature as a human person in his relationship with others, and with things, events and God. The human person develops when one acknowledges the mutual claims persons have on one another. In this way, we, our society and the world will grow to maturity.

Encounter with another takes us beyond the relationship. Besides discovering ourselves and finding our identity through involvement, we also learn the meaning of the first and the greatest commandment: love God with your whole heart, soul and mind. Although it is the first law of the christian, its meaning is found only in the experience of human love and friendship. While discovering the dimensions of another, we discover that there is the Other. We share in a love greater than we can give, a love that is greater than our friends can show, a love that calls us beyond everything. Our love and our friends' love is a shadow of this greater love, which is God.

However, to discover this love, we must experience human love. We must learn to encounter the other in dialogue. Without this, there is no Divine experience.

No one has ever seen God;
but as long as we love one another
God will live in us
and his love will be complete in us.
. . . God is love
and anyone who lives in love lives in God,
and God lives in him.
. . . We are to love then,
because he loved us first.
Anyone who says, "I love God,"
and hates his brother,
is a liar,
since a man who does not love the brother
that he can see
cannot love God, whom he has never
seen.
(1 Jn. 4:12-20)

## DISCUSSION QUESTIONS

1. What trends make it possible to compare present history to adolescent development?

2. Can the personalist movement be validly identified with the commandment of love as preached by Christ? Why or why not?

3. Is christian maturity a special kind of human maturity? Explain.

4. Discuss the qualities of maturity in a person you admire.

5. Why can friendship be called a risk?

6. Why is it necessary to experience human love before we can love God?

# Two

# MISTAKEN ENCOUNTER

Admittedly, involvement with others is important for our personal growth and for finding our identity. It is also necessary for christian living. The question remains: How do we go about it? Friendship, so basic to human growth, is a very difficult art. Because of it's difficulty and the energy it takes, many never find it. Others get lost, or give up never to experience the richest aspect of true human living. What is true encounter? What is true dialogue with another?

Dialogue is not mere conversation. It is not the exchange of conversation as in a play or a novel. Although a brilliant conversation may be informative, it remains on a superficial level. The participants in

the conversation are not affected very deeply; they are not changed. They leave with the same convictions, even perhaps confirmed in their prejudice. Conversationalists are not touched in the depth of their being. Although conversation may be concerned with serious problems, it remains on the level of opinion or simple information.

Because he is a brilliant conversationalist, a young man may be invited to more dinner parties than he can accept. He is up to date on the latest topics in politics, art, literature and social gossip. Although hostesses may vie with one another to have him on their guest list, he may not have a friend in the world. This young man prepares well for social events. He reads *Time, Newsweek* and a number of daily papers. He thinks of the right questions to ask the other guests and then lectures them on the events of the universe. This young man may be interesting, but after the conversation he and the other guests are no more changed than the performers in a play who parrot memorized lines. He reports facts and editorializes.

He may be polite and very tolerant of the opinions of others. He may be courteous, not because he respects the ideas of others, but because this is the thing to do in society. And he can afford to be tolerant, because he has nothing to lose. If his arguments are attacked, he cannot be hurt; after all, the ideas were not his. The conversation does not involve him as a person. He is not a part of it nor of the people with whom he speaks.

There is no deep encounter with another in conversation. A person may engage in discussion, not to communicate anything, nor learn anything, nor influence anyone. Conversation can be merely a tool to make an impression, to bolster one's self-image.

A heated discussion on the value of the Peace Corps may be mistaken for a true dialogue, an authentic encounter, with another. Dialectic is not geared to understanding another person. Its purpose is to learn facts, to vindicate one's own position, to win an argument. Dialectic focuses on logical truth; it shares facts, not persons. It ignores the total point of view. A rigid argument forgets that an abstract formulation of a given point cannot exhaust the total reality of sweat, blood and tears which is the lifeline of living.

Rational argument ignores the real world. Dialectic is the tool for debate to express thoughts in a pointed way. The debater strikes home as sharply as he can to devastate his opponent. In debate, the other is an object to be destroyed; therefore, the debater cannot have an explicit regard for him as a person. He moves aggressively. He must present himself as an authority or lose his case.

On the other hand, true dialogue is not aggressive, it is not authoritative, it is not out to conquer. Dialogue manifests authority through charity and concern for the other. Its power comes from genuine interest in the other. Dialogue permits the other the freedom to choose rather than drive him into a corner. It does not command and it does not impose on another's right to an opinion. Violence has no place in dialogue; its methods are peaceful. The victory of dialogue is found not through force, but in sharing and mutual enlightenment.

Frequently, dialogue is mistaken for discussion or for the methods of group dynamics. Dialogue is not a technique or a tool. Role-playing or brainstorming can be helpful in initiating dialogue (see the Epilogue). However, such a technique and methods succeed only in generating a kind of discussion. True dialogue is more than a method or a technique. Technique is used to interest a customer in buying a product, but salesmanship is not the product. Dialogue, the product, involves persons totally.

Monologue certainly is never dialogue. In this mistaken dialogue, the participants do not really have each other in mind. The other comes into play only as a sounding board, not as a real person. The other is assigned a completely passive role; he is like a sponge. The monologist expects nothing from the other except an occasional grunt of agreement, a nod of encouragement, a monosyllable to be worthy of his existence. The speaker in a monologue is only preoccupied with himself, and others have the privilege of hearing him. He loses touch with those to whom he is speaking.

The monological speaker loves to hear his own voice. He can revel in his own emotions. He excites himself. He enjoys the effects he is producing in himself and expects the same in others. He thinks others are as enthralled with what he says as he is himself. He is impressed himself with his brilliant thoughts. He is the essence of boredom.

He is a dramatist who casts himself in all sorts of roles for his own benefit. He stands before himself in power and glory to impress himself and to create an image other than his real self. His dramatic gestures, his studied attitude and his deliberate choice of words all create an effect, no matter how unreal or inauthentic. He poses before himself to live in a world of which he alone is master.

A monologue may be the result of shyness and self-consciousness. At her first fashionable cocktail party, a girl may feel very uncomfortable and unsure of herself. She may suddenly get the feeling that people are staring at her. Perhaps her slip is showing, perhaps her hair is askew, perhaps her neckline is too low, perhaps some have noticed that she really doesn't care for martinis. If one of the other guests tries to put her at ease with a few words, she immediately becomes suspicious. She does not find herself entering into direct relation with her new acquaintance. The questioner is not a person to her, but a threat. Why is he talking to me? What does he want? I can't trust him! The girl adopts a very defensive attitude. She can have no encounter with the other guest. She is on her guard. She does not permit dialogue. She has withdrawn into a monologue. The monologue is not verbalized, but carried on within herself, quietly, agonizingly.

Preoccupation with self may be called individuality, whereas personhood develops through preoccupation with others. An individual trapped in himself is not present to other persons, because he is trapped inside himself. He has a subject-object relationship; he relates indirectly to others. In this sort of relationship, the individual is very much aware of being the subject that experiences and that uses the other.

The difference between an individual and person is that the individual *associates*, whereas the person *communicates*. No one is pure person or pure individual consistently. But the more a person lets himself be mastered by individuality, the deeper he sinks into himself and the world of his own creation. The more he becomes an individual, the greater the preoccupation with talking to self, daydreaming, projection.

We Americans are especially subject to being monological people. After all, our idol is the rugged individual! We model ourselves after the frontiersmen who had to stand alone, who had to carve civilization out of virgin forests and untamed plains. Whereas the frontiersmen had to be individuals because they were alone in the wilderness, our problem is certainly the opposite.

The spirit of aggression, the spirit of conquest, the spirit of the frontier is no longer feasible in an age when we rub elbows with other men in every endeavor of life. We cannot afford mere associations only to forget our acquaintances the next day. Our lives are intertwined with others. We must share, we must communicate.

Monologue does not take the other person seriously. It does not really understand who the other is or even that he exists. The monological person takes only himself seriously. Although there is conversation with others, there is no presence to others. He responds only partially, not with his whole person. He is off in his own world, a world which is safe and where he does not have to face the challenge of the other.

He may lead people to expect a response in friendship, but later he does not follow through. He does not say what he really means and does not do what he says. This is not because he is a liar, but simply because he does not realize the consequences of his actions and his words. Because he has constructed his own world, reality must conform to his picture of himself. Thus he thinks that others also see him this way. Because he does not take others seriously, he expects that others do not take him seriously.

Monologue uses people; it exploits them. It does not comprehend the other as a person to be related to. The other person is an object to be manipulated for the monologist's own purposes. Others exist only to serve him and to bolster his ego. In effect, he obliterates others and depersonalizes them. He reduces others to the status of things. He values and deals with them in terms of their function or their usefulness to him. He uses them as a mirror to reflect his own image, as an amplifier to project his own voice.

For example, in desiring all that is best for their children, some parents want their children to be mirrors of their vanity. They want their children to be the brightest in school. Children must look right and do the right things so they will not bring disgrace to their family. A father may force his son to play football because he himself never could. A mother may want her daughter to date the boy down the block, because his family has the right connections. Such parents are not aware of their children as persons. Rather, they see their children as useful objects.

Such an exploitation of people need not be a conscious phenomenon. As one moves toward a new experience in human relationships, he is in danger of absolutizing them too soon and romanticizing them too sentimentally. A young person especially may fall into this trap. Inexperience and immaturity can sometimes lead into exclusive relationships that become occasions for mutual exploitations or a subtle self-seeking. Such relationships turn in on themselves in frustration.

Admittedly, this is a danger in personalism. However, it is well worth the risk. If a person is to mature in dialogue with others, he must be allowed to make mistakes. Above all must a young person go through the stages of social awareness. He can move into the openness of dialogue only with difficulty and by passing through the subtleties of monologue.

Monologue is not open to the views of others. For the monological man, dialogue means the opportunity to convince others that he is right. He is convinced that he has a monopoly on truth. Others are in error and he must correct them and bring them around to his way of thinking. He cannot give an inch and cannot move

toward the other; the other must come to him and depend on him.

Tho man of monologue is immobile, proud, self-righteous, dogmatic. His mind is made up before he enters into a discussion. He will not change his views. Others cannot influence him. If he is confronted with facts against his argument, he will merely brush them aside. Such a man poisons all discussion because he will always have the last word.

Finally, the monological man manifests his preoccupation with self by not paying attention to meanings, experiences, feelings and understandings that others bring to a meeting with him. Each person that comes to him is the same as the previous one, because he fails to listen between the lines. He fails to see the nuances of emotion that are spoken with the words. The joy or the agony expressed, the reaching out for understanding and sympathy—all are missed.

Because the monological man fails to penetrate into the thoughts and feelings of others, his attempts at communication are doomed to failure.

The monological man, therefore, is trapped within himself. He cannot be self-giving because he does not know how to share. He cannot love another, because he selfishly loves himself. He cannot understand another, because he cannot listen. Defense mechanisms guard him against the world outside himself. It takes the initiative of someone else to tear down the screen that blocks full experience with reality. Otherwise, the world of interpersonal relationships is closed to him. Without the help of someone else, he can never be aware of the value of others.

What is true dialogue and authentic encounter with another person? How can we escape the monological trap in which we are caught? Or how can we help others to escape from it?

## DISCUSSION QUESTIONS

1. Give your impressions of the interaction in the group. Are the discussions conversation, dialectic, monologue or dialogue?

2. How do you incorporate the shy persons in your group? What are some possible ways of involving them?

3. Why is *rugged individualism* no longer an adequate attitude for our times?

4. What are some of the techniques a monological person uses to protect himself from others?

5. Why is the interest and concern of another necessary to tear down the screens and facades of a monological person?

# Three

# AUTHENTIC ENCOUNTER

When we ask about authentic encounter, we are really asking about the nature of man. In fact, the contemporary concern for dialogue grew out of the larger interest to understand man. Existentialist philosophers have defined man as the open existent, the light or consciousness through which being reveals itself.

Man is the one who gives meaning to things. He is the shepherd of everything that exists around him. He gives the world and history direction, meaning, orientation and purpose. In using the things that surround him and in shaping the environment in which he lives, he also reveals and unfolds himself. He develops and grows into full humanity through his use of other things and, above all, through encounter with other persons.

Human existence is a paradox. He who lays down his life for others will find life. In sharing ourselves with others and giving generously of ourselves to another, we discover ourselves and have life more abundantly. Human life is essentially co-existence—living with others. Man is constituted through others. The more man conjoins his life to others, the more he finds himself.

Central to human existence is man's relationship to man. The more a person is united to another, the more he becomes a person. Outside an interpersonal relationship, the individual exists, but not a person. Selfhood, personhood, existence and meaning are all defined in terms of union with others.

By understanding our effects on the environment and our influence on relationships with others, we come to define ourselves. The shaping of self is the product of social encounter. The self-concept of each individual is circumscribed by the relationships of others and the action of the environment. The self-image or identity is shaped through interaction with others and the life situation.

However, before a person is capable of evaluating his relationships and his effects on the environment, the foundation for identity has already been laid. In the young years the self-image is shaped by the frowns of disapproval and the smiles of approval of important persons in a child's life. If others consistently react negatively to him, he will without doubt develop a poor self-image. He will begin to question *his* self-worth. His capabilities and potential may be undermined. He will lack the courage of his own convictions. But if a child meets with approval and praise when he deserves it, he will learn to respect himself, to be confident, to appreciate his worth.

The self-image, which a child develops before he is capable of understanding his relationships to others and the effects of his environment upon him, will color his attitudes later in life.

However, it is not until authentic encounter that a person will be able to cor-

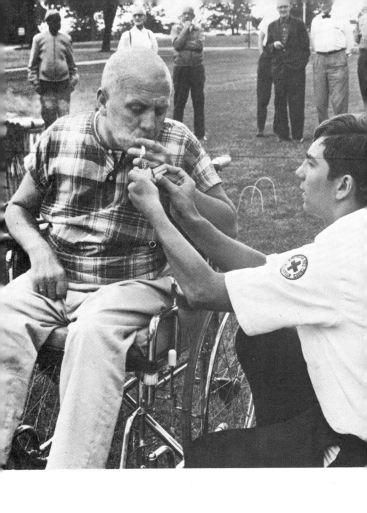

rect a mistaken self-image. In the discovery of another person, the individual meets a measure for himself. He meets a mirror in which he discovers himself and can thereby judge his true self-worth. In the rich experience of love, the world, other people and self take on new meaning and value. Life becomes full. What was drab yesterday is brilliant today.

In the experience of friendship, the person discovers himself and a purpose for life. In such an encounter the self is tested —it gives totally of itself only to discover that there is more to give.

Dialogue, authentic encounter, is essentially interpersonal relationship. The relationship, however, is only the method or the way that leads to authentic communication. Dialogue must not, therefore, be confused with just any interpersonal relationship. Dialogue is a particular kind of interpersonal relationship. What makes dialogue unique is that it is *the response of one's whole being to the otherness of the other*.

Otherness is only comprehended when a person opens himself to the other in the present concrete situation. When I accept another as he is at this moment, when I respond to his needs, his emotions, his attitudes, I encounter him. Even though I am not even conscious of the other's state of being, but nonetheless respond to him, I encounter the other. This encounter may be expressed through a word, a gesture, a smile, a glance.

Fundamentally, dialogue is the expression of an attitude. The attitude is one of being-for and being-with the other. The basic attitude that must be conveyed is that I exist for the other person and that my objective is to exist with him. It is the attitude of my willingness to share myself, of being open to the other.

At first, dialogue may be an intellectual experience: an exchange of ideas which broadens the field of our thinking. Dialogue may also be the culmination of an effective experience, which is the relationship between conscious beings. It can be described in many ways and consists of many elements. Its outstanding quality is a mutual encounter leading to communion, which is primarily inner and invisible.

Dialogue demands that the partners listen to one another and take the risk of reciprocal openness and presence to one another. Only in such a situation can there be a real flow of meaning between them. The partners in dialogue must also accept and confirm one another. They must go out to each other and experience one another while yet maintaining their own identity. Acceptance of responsibility is also necessary for dialogue. If these elements are present, then dialogue will result in the most beautiful of all human realities: the creative and enriching growth of a person moving toward greater wholeness.

Let us look closer at the elements required for dialogue.

Dialogue, according to Martin Buber, the renowned Jewish theologian, is an *I-Thou* relationship. It is a relationship of openness and mutuality between person and person.

In one sense, man can have an *I-Thou* relationship with a cat, a tree, or even a painting. Therefore the difference in an *I-Thou* relationship is not whether one relates to another human or a nonhuman object. What is decisive is the relationship itself.

If the relationship is characterized by mutuality, directness, intensity, and presence, then the relationship is *I-Thou*. In this case the relationship is valued in itself and is not only a means to an end. If the relationship is characterized by possessiveness, exploitation, and indirectness, then the relationship is *I-It*. Such a relationship is simply a means to an end.

Therefore, the *Thou* of the *I-Thou* could well be a French poodle or a Rembrandt, where an object is given the status of person, whereas the *It* of the *I-It* is often one's wife, neighbor, or even God, because they are reduced to the status of things.

Our melancholy fate is that every *Thou* in our world must at times become an *It*. It is not always possible to remain in an unbroken relationship of persons. Even our friends must be used at times. Circumstances in our life are such that at times some persons must be used, others must be ignored.

Nonetheless, the *I-Thou* and the *I-It* should alternate. The world of the *It* must be brought into the world of the *Thou*. Certainly the *Thou* must dominate when dealing with persons. As long as such alternations continue, man's existence is authentic. Without *It* relationships we could not live.

Things are necessary for the civilized ordering and structure of the world and society. But if objects were to swell up and block our return to persons, then our existence would become inauthentic and unhealthy. Things should serve and foster personal relationships. We would slip out of the *I-Thou* of dialogue into monologue, where the *I-It* predominates. We would not be human, for only dialogue humanizes.

Although *I-Thou* relationships are possible with nonhuman realities, our concern is with those that are interhuman. In interhuman relationships, the partners are neither two nor one. The partners interact; each one becomes more deeply himself as he moves to respond more fully to the other. Each becomes more conscious of being a person as he enters into relationship with the *Thou* of the other; each communicates himself.

Man becomes a real I, an authentic person, only to the extent that he does enter into relationships with others. Dialogue is this relationship between persons. Without dialogue individuals and community are abstractions.

The life of dialogue does not necessarily require that one have *much* to do with others, but that he *really* have to do with those with whom he is concerned. Much dialogue really can take place in silence, whereas much conversation is really monologue.

Nor can dialogue only take place with those whom one knows well. It is possible with complete strangers, in an unexpected moment, even in passing at a busy airport, at a sidewalk sale.

Dialogue can also be described as a mutual encounter. It is the creative opposition of two human beings involving not just their rationality, but their whole persons: their intellect and their emotions, their attitudes and their feelings. Such an involvement leads to communion. Two persons are brought together through their attitudes of mutual giving into a conscious participation of spirit and life. What happens is much more than an exchange of ideas. As each opens himself to the other, he becomes internal to the other, a taking of all that is taken in.

In dialogue, the other's appeal is for communion: "Be with me." It is a call upon the partner's being, upon what he is, not what he has. If, therefore, he should reply to the invitation with, "Be satisfied with what I have," there can be no communion, no dialogue. He would be locking himself into his private world. In his world he hopes not to be disturbed.

The communion engendered by dialogue is primarily an inner and invisible reality. There are two moments in dialogue. One moment is apparent and visible; it consists of external signs such as words, looks, gestures. The other moment, the more important, is inward and invisible; it is the true communion or encounter of persons.

The second could not come about without the first, but the first has no value in dialogue except as an invitation to communion or an expression of union. Although the living word remains the chief instrument of personal dialogue, the inner reality which the word seeks to express is by far the more important.

In *The Little Prince*, Antoine de Saint-Exupery, has the fox give the little prince a secret that he wants him to remember forever: ". . . here is my secret, a very simple secret: It is only with the heart that one can see rightly; what is essential is invisible to the eye. . . . Men have forgotten this truth. . . . You must not forget it" (New York: Harcourt, Brace and World, 1943, pp. 70,71).

And the little prince does not forget. Later, in his last conversation with the narrator: " 'The men where you live,' said the little prince, 'raise five thousand roses in the same garden—and they do not find in it what they are looking for. . . . And yet what they are looking for could be found in one single rose, or in a little water. . . . But the eyes are blind. One must look with the heart' " (p. 79).

Through dialogue, people are lifted out of themselves and are linked with one another. Even in certain, casual encounters, a touch of genuine interest can break through by means of the tone of the voice or an expression of understanding.

Earlier in this chapter we mentioned that, through the risk of reciprocal openness and presence to one another can there be a flow of meaning between the partners in dialogue. It is precisely between persons, and not within each one, that the value of dialogue lies. Man realizes his humanity and becomes what he ought to be in his meetings with other men and with the world.

What happens in the soul of each partner, whatever the psychological dynamics of each individual, is only a consequence of dialogue, for real dialogue is not to be found in one of the two partners nor in their sum. The meaning of dialogue can only be found between the partners.

While the attitude for dialogue is within persons, dialogue itself does not exist *in* persons but *between* them. What is unique to the world of man is that something can take place between persons of which language is only the sign. Through dialogue man is man with and for man. One person turns to another person as other to communicate with him in a common sphere which is different from the sphere of either one.

Each partner becomes the creature of what takes place between himself and the other. What takes place cannot be reduced to their sum or to merely programmed psychological reactions. The dialogue that results gives the highest form of self-knowledge. This self-knowledge arises from the most intimate knowledge of each other. Self-confidence increases through the confidence in the relationship, through the communion between the partners.

Anything that keeps relationship from forming between persons is a barrier to dialogue. The most basic barrier is the need and concern that every man experiences for his own being. Each individual is concerned about the preservation and the enhancement of the self. We need to adjust and fortify ourselves against the environment in which we live. We must cope with known and unknown threats against our well-being. If we do not do this successfully, we live in constant anxiety and insecurity. Driven by anxiety we look for assurances that will give us courage to be and to accept and to love ourselves.

Such a search for self-affirmation leads to a paradoxial way of behavior. At times we will draw close to others; at times we will alienate ourselves from them. Usually, the search for security makes us run. Once running, it is difficult to stop and evaluate our situations and another. A person who is constantly concerned with himself cannot really stop to look at anyone else; he is always rushing through life. Hence he never learns to understand himself or anyone else.

Among the many barriers to dialogue are five principal ones: deception, language, preconceptions, intolerance, and defensiveness.

Deception is really trying to be something we are not. Many people attempt to live behind a facade so that their true self cannot shine forth. Human existence can proceed from what one truly is not or from what one wishes to seem. The two modes mix in every man, for all of us have mixed motivation. But one or the other will predominate. The person who lives by what

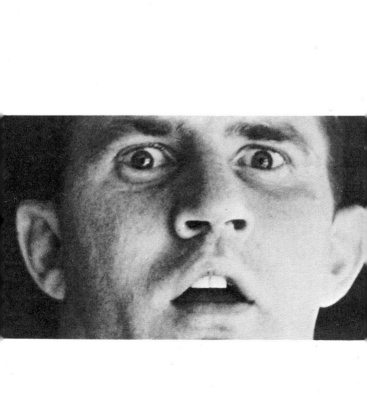

he really is may try to influence others, but his primary concern is not the impression he is making on them. He does not try to appear artificial to gain prestige or approval. The man who tries to be other than what he is, is calculating. He is concerned primarily with the effects his words will have on others. He wants so badly to be accepted that he would affect interest. He becomes a master at deception.

Language is another barrier to dialogue. Words are the usual way we transfer thought from one mind to another. However, the problem with words is that they are given shape and color by the life situation of each man. The same words will have different meanings for different persons. Differences of sex, age, social status, environment, profession, personal history, character, thought patterns, experiences, perception of self, views about others—all are elements which impregnate language with nuances. Children do not understand their parents; parents do not understand their children. Therefore, language can hamper the effective communication so necessary for dialogue.

Closely related to the language problem are our preconceptions. Every person is born in a particular culture and stems from a particular family background. Since there are so few human instincts, if any, the individual is shaped by his experience in this environment. Some of these experiences are common to all people in a particular culture. But even these are filtered through the individual's unique biological organism.

The result is that no two individuals have exactly the same environment, either physically or culturally. Each person undergoes slightly different experiences from his birth on. To add to the complication, later experiences are influenced by the earlier ones. As a result, the variation in perception of the identical physical phenomenon grows wider and wider between individuals as time goes on. Preconceptions, then, can be destructive.

Thus, each person has his own set of preconceptions and images. Each carries his own meaning to an encounter. In attempted dialogue many misunderstandings and distortions result because of these presuppositions and the difference of nuance in language.

A fourth barrier to dialogue is intolerance of the other's position. Frequently we want to impose our own convictions on others. We want to make our point and we do not allow someone else to explain his. We do not hear the other. He might possess the truth and be willing to share it, but we do not allow him. All the other is expected to do is to listen to our reasoning and eventually capitulate.

If we enter into dialogue with an unbending intolerance of other views, our minds will be closed whenever an opposing fact or opinion enters on the scene. We will react by saying that the new ideas unnecessarily rock the boat or that they will get us nowhere or that they are a waste of time. We enter the dialogue to conquer, rather than to serve. In doing so we kill any possibility of real dialogue.

Defensiveness is the final key barrier to dialogue. We fear being hurt and so build a wall around ourselves. We crawl into a shell and do not allow others to reach our inner being. Reuel L. Howe sums it up:

... Experience in relationships ... are various ... we bring not only trust, but also mistrust, of other people. We bring not only our desire for love, but our fear of love because some of our experiences with family and friends have hurt us. We bring the resentments toward people that we have accumulated as a result of what we believe their injustices to be. We bring our defensive ways of living that help to keep demanding, hurtful people at a safe distance. We bring our image to ourselves and others, and using them like puppets, vainly try to act out our concerns. We are afraid to let people see us, and we are afraid to see others really. We put on masks these masks, in reality, keep us from being found (*The Creative Years* [New York: Seabury Press, 1959], p. 70).

In this chapter, we have tried to point out that dialogue is not mere conversation, friendly discussion. Neither is dialogue monologue in which one is so preoccupied with himself that he either fails to take the other seriously or actually seeks to exploit him.

Genuine dialogue is a special kind of interpersonal relationship which can best be described as *encounter* or *communion*. Precisely because it is a relationship, it is an inward, invisible reality. Unfortunately, many of us tend to confuse it with its outward signs and expressions. Dialogue is an attitude, a state of being, a communion. It is a marvelous experience that can unleash our creative powers if we do not allow barriers to get in the way.

## DISCUSSION QUESTIONS

1. Explain the definition: Man is the open existent, the consciousness through which being reveals itself.

2. If we share ourselves, how is it true that we grow as persons?

3. What is your self-image? How does this compare with the way others see you? How authentic is each one?

4. Discuss in detail the attitude necessary for dialogue.

5. List some relationships that are *I-It*. How can these be transformed into *I-Thou* relationships?

# Four

# WHY DIALOGUE?

Why dialogue? It is much easier to merely live in a world of our own and not seek involvement with others. It is nice to have friends, but to actively involve ourselves with others is against our inclination. Yet earlier we mentioned that dialogue is with others—dialogue is the very nature of man.

Dialogue between man and man is a meeting between God and man. God reveals himself in relationships of persons. After all, the very meaning of the incarnation is that God is personal and found in time and history. By identifying himself with man, Christ made possible the encounter of God in man and the real association of persons.

Dialogue between men provides the context in which the love of God is present and through which the Spirit of God is free to work his powerful transformation. Christ himself worked through this relationship. He was open; he was vulnerable; he was available. He offered his friendship to every man, and those who accepted his offer were changed in the core of their being—love transforms, love redeems.

A man full of leprosy asked, "Lord, if you will, you can make me clean." Christ simply touched the man and said, "I will; be clean" (Lk. 5:12-13). Another time Christ was passing the tax collector, Levi, and he said to him, "Follow me." Levi accepted the invitation and left everything to begin a new way of life (Lk. 5:27-28). From all over the Near East, people came to hear him and to be cured of their diseases, because power came forth from him and he healed all (Lk. 6:17-19). "No longer do I call you servants, but friends. Love one another as I have loved you" (Jn. 15:15).

In these few examples, we see that those who accepted Christ's gift of himself were transformed radically. Through all his relationships, Jesus taught that the gift of self is integral to the passover from the human to the divine. This is the way God wants men to come to him.

Through our total giving of self, others are not only changed, but we ourselves are changed in the root of our being. It is not possible to answer the invitations God sends without answering at the same time for other persons. Our lives are linked to others. And the lifelong invitation of salvation is extended to us through others. To renounce human life is to misunderstand God completely. People are not hurdles on the road to God; they are the road.

However intense our private devotions, however satisfying our liturgical services, however strong our faith, if they are separated from love of our brother, they are meaningless. As St. Paul says, our life has the hollow ring of brass if openness is not given to our brother. Without allowing others to change our lives we will have passed over the earth like a whirlwind. Once we have passed, there is nothing to show for our life.

Another way of saying that God is discovered through our involvement with others is that God is found in community. God is found *only* in community. No one can discover God unless he seeks to build the human community. When Jesus emphasized that one loves God only in the measure that he loves his neighbor, he was saying that God comes only to those who work for community. But community happens only through dialogue—when people appreciate each other and seek authentic relationships with each other.

This in fact constitutes authentic christianity in today's world. If human beings can listen to one another and respond, christianity is alive today. In the context of a human community, the love of God and the task of love that Christ sets before us makes sense.

Not only does dialogue bring men to God; it also brings man to himself. In a dialogical relationship, a person can be himself and can allow the other to be himself. When a human being genuinely becomes a person and discovers the personhood in another, he discovers that together they make "we," a community. Therefore, the dialogical scene happens only when a man enters into relation with other persons. If there is no sharing, there is no man. Man becomes man not by seeking himself, but by seeking others. He becomes whole, not by closing in on himself, but by opening up to another self.

A man would not even be conscious of being a person unless he entered into relationship with another person. Without responsibility to others, the brute instincts are unleashed. His own relationship to himself is mediated by the other. Without a dialogical relationship, he would miss his meaning and existence as a man. If he chose to be monological, he would not and could not be human. He would exploit others and return to the laws of the jungle.

In monologue a person loses his destiny. Whereas another person would stand in judgment of the meaninglessness of egoism and self-centeredness, in monologue the individual sets his own unreal goal. Without the possibility of reflection in another, the person would lock himself into his own world, alone, isolated.

Jesus put it very simply: "Believe me. Unless a grain of wheat falls into the earth and dies, it remains alone. If it dies, it bears much fruit. He who loves his life loses it . . ." (Jn. 12:24-25). Unless the grain of wheat remains open to the influence outside itself (the sun, the soil, the rain), it will not grow; it will not achieve its destiny; it will not become what it ought to become.

Through genuine interest in dialogue, we die to any innate desire to withdraw from people, or to succumb to shyness and fears of involvement. We must die to our egocentricity. We must break through the shell of monologue and open out to others. With such an attitude, our total presence should beget in another the capacity to understand and accept. We will be the catalyst which activates others to grow in their humanity.

Another reason for dialogue is to give others the experience of love. Man's greatest need is to be loved. Unless he receives love, he will never be able to give himself in love; he will never be able to express himself totally.

Usually, we assume that a person has already had an unqualified experience of love as a child, from parents and from those on whom a child must depend for love. However, this is contrary to evidence. A vast number of people have not had the experience of being loved. As a result, in their image of themselves they appear alienated and without self-worth. They cannot cope with failure and suffer from feelings of inferiority. Therefore the christian, through his dialogue, can be an instrument of love. In giving such love to another, he will make it possible for the other to reach out and to give love. He has the power not only to change his own life, but also the lives of others.

Love is the gift of self to another. It is the marvelous ability to transcend oneself and give to the other all that really makes him a person: his ideas, real concern, humor, interest, warmth. But before one can give himself in such a way, he has to feel that his gift is worthwhile. He has to possess a genuine love for and an accept-ance of himself. He must feel his worth and dignity. Otherwise, his gift will seem to be an imposition on the receiver. He will think that, since he has nothing that is worth giving, the other person cannot possibly be interested in him, or enjoy his companionship, or want his friendship. The only response to such feelings would be condescending politeness, sympathy and utter boredom, none of which we appreciate.

The difficulty is that a young person who has no sense of self-value projects his poor self-concept into the minds of others. "They cannot possibly think I'm anything at all, so why inflict myself on them," he reasons. "I'll only be rejected in the end anyway."

The simple fact is that no one can love another until he first loves himself. No one can see true worth in another, until he sees worth in himself. This is where the dialogical person can help. Through genuine dialogue, he can give those who feel worthless an experience of positive, unconditional acceptance, care and love. When the other really experiences his worth reflected in another's eyes over a period of time, he will begin to feel it himself. Then, he will be enabled to love; then, he can begin to grow in the Christ-life.

Another reason for dialogue is a corollary to the one we have just mentioned; dialogue brings meaning to human existence. Through dialogue, a man can see his life as truly meaningful. The search for meaning is man's primary motivational force. Nietzsche once said: "He who has a *why* to live can bear with almost any *how*." Meaning in life comes through dialogue, through relationship.

Being together is the most meaningful experience we have. If we are with someone, a movie seems better, golf is more fun. Watching a sunset with another makes it twice as beautiful, and that is certainly true of a moonlit night. Other values derive their depths from the most basic and meaningful existence we have, namely, being with another, someone with whom we can share our experience.

Being together with others or at least doing something for someone else, brings luster to other values. Joy is born in dialogue. Also, the experience of freedom becomes real, because, paradoxically, we are truly free and independent only insofar as we acknowledge that we have a bond with other persons. From such freedom a true sense of responsibility emerges, because the opportunity to respond comes when one is first addressed in dialogue.

Life itself becomes a value through dialogue, for the true purpose of human life comes into being in authentic encounter. Life becomes worth living. Despair creeps into us when we feel we have nothing to give and no one cares. These are the feelings that lead to suicide.

Also, dialogical relationship is the force that integrates christian life. By stripping away the superficialities of life and social pressures, christianity exposed the simple message of love.

Jesus spoke of only one commandment as specifically his: "This is my commandment, that you love one another as I have loved you" (Jn. 15:12). And in his parable about the king who will come at the end of time, he tells us that those who serve his brothers are in fact, although unknowing, really serving him. He startles us with the truth that to love man is to love God (see Mt. 25:31-46). St. John develops this theme in his first letter: "He who does not love his brother whom he has seen, cannot love God whom he has not seen" (1 Jn. 4:20).

Therefore love of God and love of neighbor are not two distinct loves; they are one and the same. When I love my neighbor, in and by that very act I love God. Thus the vertical line of love for God and the horizontal line of love for man are extended simultaneously. When one line is authentically intensified, the other also grows.

Christianity comprises all aspects of human living. Human life is not lived in compartments with one section dedicated to God in prayer and liturgical worship, and another section given to work, recreation, and still another given to meeting people. If we view our life divided in such a way, only the time given to prayer and meditation belongs truly and directly to God. And asceticism is seen as primarily moral. Practice of virtue would be approached negatively; it would consist of a struggle against everything sinful and against all the dangerous powers of human nature and of the wicked world.

Rather, the christian vision of life integrates. Everything and everyone is an occasion for meeting God. However, encounter with God depends on a dialogical attitude toward life. In other words, if I have made the fundamental option to abandon monologue and to run the risk of openness to all reality and especially toward persons, my life takes on a transcendent aspect. As reality unfolds before me now and as I concern myself with persons now, I meet God.

In this vision, christian asceticism is not withdrawal, but presence—a radical openness to and acceptance of persons, tasks or events that confront me. This view is utterly different from quietism, which would see God as manipulating events and man as passively accepting what God does. Man is not resigned, but creative. Man seizes each moment as the expression and the sacrament of God. The concrete circumstance which I choose or which happens to me, this person who comes to me, are my opportunity to reach out and meet God. My asceticism consists in being actively and creatively *there*. I am present, responsible, available, vulnerable to the risks necessarily involved in living.

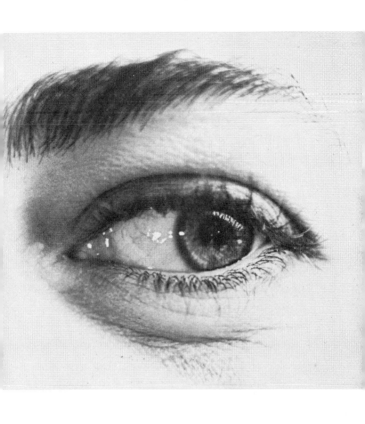

Prayer, too, takes the form of response to the moment. Prayer can be an invitation to express gratitude, or to ask for help from God, or experience joy in him, or to search for meaning over a more extended period of time. And I respond to such invitations only through the grace and power of Jesus Christ and in his Holy Spirit.

Christian living is a dialogue among God, others, the world and myself. The life of dialogue is the life that Jesus Christ lived and preached. To opt, then, for a dialogical orientation is to aim straight at the heart of christianity.

Another reason for dialogue is one which pertains more to its means or method than specifically to the relationship itself. A dialogical attitude can lead us to a fuller view of truth. It reveals the comprehensive and related character of truth. It reveals truth in its many dimensions.

No one man has a full grasp of truth. Each man with an honest conviction has at least a portion of the truth. There is no such thing in concrete reality as pure error. Every error contains some particle or manifestation of truth, and every truth is hampered by the limitations of our human understanding. The irreplaceable function of the dialogical method is to facilitate the confrontation of diverse points of view within an atmosphere of acceptance and understanding.

In dialogue different ways of looking at reality qualify and supplement one another. Thereby they provide a comprehensive view that is more completely the truth than any one of them separately. Each one of us possesses truth, but we must set this truth in relation with the truth which others possess so that the full dimension may be revealed.

Dialogue avoids the danger of selectivity and subjectivity. Too frequently we fix exclusively on one aspect of the truth. In doing so we obscure or forget other aspects which are equally or more important.

Through dialogue a man opens himself to an insight, interpretation and meaning that is greater and more profound than what could have been attained by any single contributor. The experience resulting from sincere and open dialogue brings home the truth of Christ's words, "Where two or three are gathered in my name there I am in their midst" (Mt. 18:20).

The community character of truth is particularly relevent for theological truth. For God speaks his word not primarily to the individual, but to the whole community, the church. No one person, no one structure receives the word of God. In searching for divine truth, dialogue is not a luxury but a necessity.

The dialogical or the community search for truth has two important by-products. First, it releases the individual participant's freedom and creativity. He feels himself accepted and respected as a person; he sees that his opinion and insights are valued. He experiences that no one is seeking to dominate him. As a result, in this nonthreatening atmosphere, he can unlock his repressed creativity and rid himself of monological tendencies.

The second by-product of the dialogical search for truth is that the very effort makes each participant feel the truth to be his truth and not just a string of words accepted on the authority of someone else.

Therefore each person is made a unique possessor through the communal search. What he learns will make a difference in his life, and not just in his ideas.

This chapter has given six reason why it is important that we dialogue. Through the dialogical relationship, each one of us is brought to God, for God reveals himself through the relationships of man with man. Through dialogue God became human; through dialogue man becomes divine.

Secondly, dialogue also brings man to himself and enables him to become not just an individual, but a person. In dialogue, the individual becomes conscious of his personhood. He creates his person through openness and in genuine relationship with other men.

A third reason for dialogue is that a dialogical person gives others the experience of love, which is man's greatest need. Without an experience of love, a person develops a poor self-image and, therefore, that person will not be able to break out of himself in order to love. He in turn will not be able to love. Hence, growth in Christian life is stifled.

Fourthly, dialogue brings meaning to man's life. Psychologists and philosophers agree that relationship with others is the most meaningful experience man can know. Dialogue enables us to respond with joy and freedom to the demands of life.

Dialogue, fifthly, demonstrates that the christian life should be integrated around the reality of loving relationships. To love man *is* to love God. Prayer, asceticism, and a radical option are all seen as the willingness to take the risk of openness. They are a total response to a person or an event that meets me now, for God meets me in them.

The final reason is that dialogue leads to a fuller understanding of truth than could be reached by any man alone. When the insights of one are brought into relation with the insights of another, the result is a more comprehensive view of truth. Through this dialogical experience, the participants can come to a deeper appreciation of the value and meaning of community, to a realization of their own creative powers, and to the realization that the truth uncovered is truth for their lives.

Although we might be convinced that dialogue is important, how do we dialogue? How do we enter into dialogical relationship with others? The next two chapters will deal with these questions.

## DISCUSSION QUESTIONS

1. How does the incarnation of the Word make dialogue between man and God possible?

2. Practically, how does salvation come to us through others? How is God found in community?

3. How does dialogue aid us to grow? How does it help to realize our destiny?

4. Why is self-love a necessary prelude to loving others?

5. Discuss how the christian vision of life integrates our personality.

# Five

# ATTITUDE IN APPROACH

There are two possible approaches to dialogue. One approach deals more directly with the life of dialogue and is therefore attitudinal. The other approach deals more directly with the technique of dialogue and is therefore more practical in approach. This chapter will discuss the attitude in approach.

A person can be dialogical only if he adopts definite attitudes, certain ways of thinking and acting. Any dichotomy between thought and action, of course, immediately establishes an obstacle to dialogue. What the person *is* is primary, for what he does and says flows from him as person. In dialogue the person himself is the chief medium of his message. In fact, the person himself is the message and in many ways is more important than the message itself.

We can preach the love and charity of Christ, but if this very concern is not conveyed by our being, we are not convincing. We are not witnesses to what we believe or profess. Rather, we are the whitened sepulchers that appear beautiful on the outside, but inside are filled with decay. Therefore, a person who uses dialogical, or relational, language must convey the meaning behind his words by his person.

Such an attitude demands constant effort. The dialogical person must have the courage to be open and warm, interested and concerned. He must constantly strive to be what he professes in faith. In living what he insists on being, the dialogical person helps others to change their life. By extending his love, the dialogical person begets love in others, and, as was mentioned in the previous chapter, helps others to transcend themselves for authentic christian living.

The paradoxical effect of dialogical living is that, when a person tries to live altruistically, he discovers in himself an astonishing ability to be increasingly self-giving, understanding and loving. Undoubtedly there is a fear that we may not all be capable of openness.

Yet dialogue is not a talent given to some and not to others. It does not require that one be an extrovert. It does not depend on a keen intellect nor on a certain emotional composition; it does not depend on the biological structure nor on the body's chemistry. Dialogue is not a charism.

*Being a dialogical person depends solely on whether or not we want to give ourselves or withhold ourselves.* Do we want to share? Dialogue can only come into existence when a person decides to give himself. Dialogue then becomes his power to be a creator of himself and of others.

This is a point frequently forgotten. Both persons in a relationship are in process. Each one is growing, each one is changing, each is searching for himself. Consequently the relationship must also be dynamic. As the persons create themselves, they also create each other through a relationship that is in process.

Approaching dialogue with this attitude helps us to put up with someone else's fickleness, moods and inconsistency. After all, growth, while it is constant in principle, takes place through stops and starts. Therefore dialogue must be approached as being in process, because the persons involved are in process. Dialogue is dynamic, because the persons are creative.

Dialogue is in everyone's reach, if only each one decides to give and not hold back. The decision to remain monological or become dialogical is the foundation on which all other means of dialogue are based. The question is, then, are we willing? We must make a decision.

Once we have made this decision we can move on to consider the other means which are the necessary conditions for the life of dialogue.

The first condition for dialogue is *openness*. The dialogical person is one who is open to the other side. He has learned to temper his preoccupation with himself— with his human respect, his shyness, his nervousness, with his concern over how he looks or sounds. He respects the opinions and convictions of others and is willing to respond to the meaning they communicate. The dialogical man is a man who listens. He is a man who is present to his partner. He is attentive to the other.

True listening demands full attentiveness. It is easy to appear attentive and friendly and yet not really be present. A true listener hears not only words and ideas; he also hears the heartbeat, the emotional tone; he hears what the words are trying to convey but do not fully express.

Listening to the other is really the first obligation one assumes after deciding to become dialogical. Learning to listen to others is the beginning of love. A person who does not develop patient and long listening, will soon be talking beside the point and not really addressing himself to the other.

Because we are so interested in ourselves, we usually listen with half an ear; we just wait for the other person to finish, for we already know what he has to say. We are polite enough to let him finish, but we are impatient, inattentive. We are biding our time so we can present our arguments and reasons to conquer him. This is not listening, nor fulfilling the first obligation of love. Therefore, it is directly against the proper attitude of dialogue.

Dialogue cannot take place unless openness and presence are *reciprocal.* Since dialogue is communion, it demands mutual giving, the second condition for dialogue. In dialogue two persons must be turned toward one another.

Reciprocity means accepting fully the presence of another while at the same time one opens himself freely to the other's influence. The result is a mutual modification in the depths of each one. My presence and openness to another help him to be open and present to me and vice versa. Reciprocity is truly a case of each life open to the other so that each partner experiences the being of the other in the mystery of his own. Both share; both listen; both speak; both are changed.

This kind of openness involves risk. It involves the risk of being hurt. For in dialogue the other person retains the freedom to reject. He may choose to refuse the offer of friendship. When one is willing to enter into the area of relationship, he also accepts this vulnerability. This means that dialogue is a delicate, demanding and perilous undertaking. The decision to be dialogical also means a commitment to the possibility of being manipulated or exploited by the very person with whom communion is sought.

Also included in this decision is the risk of pain that necessarily comes when the other partner in the dialogue must step out of one's life, perhaps forever. This is the price of becoming involved with another person. Again an illustration from *The Little Prince* brings out this risk.

So the little prince tamed the fox. And when the hour of his departure drew near —"Ah," said the fox, "I shall cry." "It is your own fault," said the little prince. "I never wished you any sort of harm: but you wanted me to tame you." ... "Yes that is so," said the fox. "But now you are going to cry!" said the little prince. "Yes that is so," said the fox. Then it has done you no good at all!" "It has done me good," said the fox, "because of the color of the wheat fields" (p. 68).

The experience of involvement is worth the risk of being hurt, because it gives life a fuller dimension.

Another kind of risk interwoven with opennness is that of not being sure of where the dialogue will lead. Real dialogue is possible only if one takes the risk of being influenced by the other. This means that genuine dialogue cannot be pre-arranged; it cannot be programmed. There must always be the element of surprise, an element of the unknown.

No one can know in advance what he should say or what he will come to understand. In dialogue, there must remain the challenge to change one's life without knowing what it will be changed to. Openness demands the kind of truth and faith that Abraham had when he set out for an unknown land. Yet God was with him on the way, and Abraham was changed as he followed.

With this guarantee, there is no certainty about where dialogue will lead. One must be prepared to reexamine his own position and to make an agonizing reappraisal of himself and of his way of life.

He must be honest and admit that he does not have all the answers. He must acknowledge his role as a fellow-seeker and not hide his own doubts and confusion. He must not be afraid to concede that he has been mistaken. If he is truly open and honest, he may have to let go of some firmly held conviction, or modify some cherished way of acting. He may come to see himself in a new, not always flattering, light. Always, dialogue is a voyage of self-discovery as well as the search for a fuller understanding of the other.

Another condition of dialogue is *understanding*. Understanding generates meaning between partners. For most people, dialogue is at first an intellectual experience. Gradually it develops into an affective union, which is the highest meaning of dialogue. A flow of meaning is essential between partners. Each must understand what the other is trying to communicate. While one attempts to understand the words the other is using, he at the same time realizes that words frequently obscure the intended meaning. Language both half reveals and half conceals.

Nothing is worthy of the name dialogue unless it is real expression of one mind to another. Authentic dialogue is the communication of meaning and the ascertaining of meaning.

A dialogical attitude demands serious involvement with the other person and a determined desire to understand him and to be understood by him. This kind of understanding means more than an intellectual quality. It is an involvement of the whole man, not just his intellect.

In dialogue a person must be aware of the other's world. He must be aware of the feelings, thoughts and experiences of the person with whom he is attempting to dialogue. Only then will meaning be shared and involvement become real.

*Acceptance* and *confirmation* must also be present in dialogue. Each person in the dialogue must be aware that the other is unique, that he is different from oneself. And I must accept him as different. Thus, real dialogue can begin only when one says to the other, "I accept you as you are, in your otherness and uniqueness." The acceptance must be complete and unconditional with no need to defend, attack, excuse or blame.

Every true existential relationship begins with acceptance. It permits the other person to feel that he is received just as he is. Confirmation adds to this, not so much the affirmation of what the person is now, but what he can become. It adds a creative element to the relationship. This can give the partner strength and courage to grow and to change. While acceptance strips away the need for defensive barriers, confirmation releases the potentialities to develop. Dialogical life, therefore, is not static but dynamic.

Still another condition of dialogue is *to experience the other person's life.* This means more than experiencing the other's psychological presence. Somehow it means including the other's total presence within myself. I am included in the other's life and he in mine. This kind of relationship presupposes that we experience a common event, and that each lives through that event from the standpoint of the other, without, however, abandoning his own viewpoint.

I truly feel what the other feels, and yet retain my own unique way of experiencing the event. I do not withdraw from the other, nor ask that he exist only as part of my experience. Rather, I try to turn fully toward him and to reach out to him through his concrete life-situation.

Dialogue also requires *distance*. There must be present a distinctness. If one person seeks to lose himself in the other, he destroys the possibility of relationship. Dialogue does not require identification, but polarity; over-identification can only bring distortion.

Two persons must maintain the uniqueness of their own person in the relationship. They must refuse any attempt at assimulation. In dialogue the partners are present to one another in their otherness, in their independence, in their self-reality, and yet responding to one another with all the power of their hearts.

The life of dialogue requires that one encounters others and yet holds his own ground in the meeting. Any abnormal dependence of one on the other or any blurring of the distance would harm the relationship and therefore the dialogue. Dialogue must always remain an *interpersonal* relationship, a relationship between persons.

Every man has the *responsibility* to be open to relationship with another. Whether or not that person responds positively to our presence is not our concern. We place our openness within the scope of his freedom to accept or reject through the grace of the Holy Spirit. We can only offer an opportunity for dialogue. The response to our invitation is not within our control. All we can do is to extend an invitation by being approachable and available. Our human and christian responsibility is to be ready to offer dialogue, to be vulnerable to other persons. If we are attracted to another person, we may hope that our gift will be accepted and fear that it will be rejected. If the other has very little attraction, we may experience our selfishness and the instinct to withdraw. However, in both cases, the obligation remains to stay and to offer ourselves for dialogue.

Once we have entered into relationship with another, only the permission of the other gives us the right to withdraw. Once we have accepted the responsibility, we cannot shirk it. Withdrawal would cause untold harm and pain to the partner. Therefore each must bear the burden of the other and see the relationship through its various stages of growth. To break off a relationship unilaterally is to retreat into monologue.

As the fox told the little prince: "But you must not forget. . . . You become responsible forever, for what you have tamed. You are responsible for your rose. . ." (de Saint-Exupery, p. 71).

The life of dialogue also requires *patience*. One must be willing to move slowly and to start where the other person is, not where he perhaps should be. He must follow the law of gradual development and not try to force the relationship to evolve faster than is possible. When the little prince asked the fox what he had to do in order to tame him, the fox answered:

> You must be very patient. . . . First you will sit down a little distance from me—like that—in the grass. I shall look at you out of the corner of my eye, and you will

say nothing. Words are the source of mis-understandings. But you will sit a little closer to me, everyday . . . (de Saint-Exupery, p. 67).

Along with patience there must be *a willingness to waste time.* A willingness to spend time with the person to whom one is offering the gift of dialogical relationship is absolutely essential. The time may be spent on nothing of consequence, but while the sharing goes on, the partners are building the relationship. Through bull sessions we come to know one another's likes and dislikes, thought patterns, problems. True dialogue often begins with casual talk; once the relationship is established it can be deepened through more casual talk. As the fox says to the little prince: "It is the time you have wasted for your rose that makes your rose so important" (de Saint-Exupery, p. 71).

Too few of us are willing to waste time. Our lives are measured by the clock; our careers depend on our usefulness. We worry about losing time. But are we not taking our careers too seriously? Are we not placing the emphasis in the wrong place? Human fulfillment comes through dialogue with persons and not through service to objects.

We must be ready to allow ourselves to be interrupted. People will constantly be crossing our path and cancelling our plans with claims, petitions. We may pass them by. When we do, we are passing by our own fulfillment, our own salvation. It is in the people that cross our lives that our salvation lies; the final question asked about our life will be how much we did for the least of the brethren.

The final condition for a life of dialogue is *prayer*. We need to ask God for the gift of openness to our brothers. As we try to live the life of dialogue, we will experience the difficulty of being vulnerable; we will grow tired of taking risks; we will feel overburdened by the many people that will put claims on our time, energy and love. We will be discouraged at times by our own weakness. Therefore we will need to trust more in the power and grace of God than in our own efforts.

Through prayer we can receive from him the strength we need to go on. In prayer we can offer the dialogue to him, leaving its fruitfulness in his hands. Also we stand in need of recognizing the moments and opportunities that are offered for dialogical living. It is all too easy to pass by the signs and directions.

Perhaps the most famous person in history who failed in dialogue was Judas, the disciple who betrayed Christ. Not able to make a commitment to the love offered him by Christ, he chose to reject the invitation to dialogue. Consequently he acted in secret; he could not be open about his actions. Even at the last supper, the other apostles thought Judas was going to give alms to the poor. Although he was trusted, he could not be open.

Because he had decided against dialogue with Christ, guilt finally overtook Judas. Aware of not having reciprocated love, he could no longer face life. And when he realized the opportunity given him, it was too late. The risk he was not willing to take brought him to his death.

Christ, on the night before his death, understood that Judas had already rejected love, but that evening offered him the choice again. And the freedom of choice led to Christ's own destruction.

Judas could not understand Christ's acceptance of him nor the relationships others had with Christ. When the woman poured perfumes over his master's feet, Judas saw it only as a misuse of money. Nor was Judas willing to accept Christ's predictions of death. That ultimate sacrifice of love was meaningless. Because he had only joined the band of twelve for personal benefit, in Christ's death he saw all of his selfish dreams collapsing. The time spent with Christ had been time wasted without gain. The invitation to dialogue had been wasted also because Judas could not give in love. But even when it was almost too late, the invitation was still extended.

In this chapter we have delineated the conditions which dialogue requires. Each one depends upon a decision to live a dialogical life which no one can force upon another. The choice to live such a life is free as is the acceptance or rejection of another's openness. However, such a life is well worth the pain, the agony and the energy it takes, for through it we find our fulfillment, we find our destiny and we live a christian life.

## DISCUSSION QUESTIONS

1. Explain the statement: the person is the medium of his message.

2. What is the basic attitude necessary for dialogue?

3. Discuss in detail the necessary conditions for dialogue. Are there any others which you think are essential?

4. How have you succeeded or failed in dialogues you have experienced? What elements were missing? What elements were present?

# Six

# DIALOGUE IN FRIENDSHIP AND COMMUNITY

How do we achieve dialogue? The obligations to dialogue arise from our desire to mature as persons. But how do we build encounter between persons? The church is struggling to rid herself of the impersonalism that has gripped her for centuries. Once again she wants to experience the community of the apostles. To create the environment for sharing, for human growth, for community, each one must make all his energies and talents available.

We have already discussed the attitudes necessary for dialogue. However, the willingness to communicate and to share with others is a far cry from the art necessary to bridge the gap between persons. Allowing others to encounter us genuinely is a lost art. The bustle of modern living is mainly concerned with getting a job done and rushing home to rest for the next busy day.

In this outlook on life, other persons become utilities for making money. They are objects to be used or enjoyed. What is interesting about them is what can be interpreted for productivity. Many graduates from college who go for their first job interviews are horrified by this approach. But there is little they can do; they either resign themselves to the machine routine or drop out of society.

If we are sincere about developing a dialogical relationship, we must learn the art of giving and taking. A relationship between people is basically a contract which must be respected by the other partner. If I am not ready to give myself completely, the other person must not demand it.

However, friendship is not a business deal. We do not set the limits and then enter into a relationship with another per-

son. The limits and/or terms of the contract entered into by friendship come from the spontaneity of life. Friendship is as limited as the person entering into it. Therefore, it is potentially infinite. But the depth of a relationship cannot be predetermined; it must develop freely and spontaneously or not at all.

Because the backgrounds of individuals vary, they may not be able to communicate on all levels. This does not compromise their relationship, although it does say something about the degree of friendship. A fact of life is that we cannot do everything with or say everything to everyone. We enjoy going to a movie with some friends; with others who seem to us more compassionate, we can share our anxieties and innermost feelings.

The human person is a strange, paradoxical creature. He cannot grow or understand his identity without being in relationship to other persons; yet he cannot preserve that unique identity without some privacy and solitude. He needs a healthy balance in his life between communication with others and quiet listening to himself, between action and contemplation. Only through that delicate blend will he be able to develop an inner strength and depth that will overflow to others. Only then will he truly communicate.

Some men and women seem very congenial at first, but after we come to know them better, we discover that they lack substance. Their communication remains on the level of chit-chat, but no personal sharing. Real dialogue between friends reaches bedrock of personal feelings and thoughts.

Nevertheless one cannot demand this inner revelation of another. After all, friendship is a free gift of self, and that freedom must not be violated. Sometimes we may feel that we are giving more and revealing more than our friend. This is a painful experience. But the life of dialogue means risking that kind of crucifixion. Friendship calls for patience. Perhaps our willingness to accept the other where he is and to move slowly in the relationship will free him. The barriers that prevent him from communicating on a deep level will tumble.

In friendship the supreme virtue is the ability to listen. Through listening one is completely open to the other person. This requires full attentiveness, total presence. This does not mean that the ears are always cocked in the direction of the other. It means that we listen with our whole person. We must hear the spoken and unspoken words, the grunts and gestures.

Openness to our friend allows us to be sensitive to the feedback. It is a check on our giving so that the other person can respond. Not allowing for adequate response will turn friendship into quicksand; we are constantly pouring out and the other person is trapped. Listening preserves the freedom of giving and responding.

Listening is far from passive. It involves a constant effort to understand. Therefore, a constant rechecking and reflection is necessary to make a friendship work.

At times two friends may feel the need to discuss their relationship. In general, this can be healthy, but care must be taken not to let artificiality creep in. A direct confrontation about the dynamics of a friendship may tend to make the partners too self-conscious and result in snuffing out spontaneity in self-giving. It may also turn the relationship back on itself too much. Friendship must be primarily a being-with, a growing together. Therefore, while a direct confrontation should not be deliberately avoided, it must never remain the central theme during all moments of companionship.

Perhaps these few reflections about the art of friendship are helpful. They are not a complete treatment on the subject, but hopefully will contribute to a deeper understanding of what friendship is and thus encourage the desire to experience it in actuality.

Just as there are aids for two people in dialogue, there are also guidelines for building friendship on a wider level, namely, community.

We might begin to build community as Christ did in Samaria. He somehow had to overcome their prejudice. So he decided to go to a spot where everyone in the village eventually had to come—the well. Sitting down, he made himself available to anyone interested in exchanging gossip. Eventually a woman came along and he asked her for a drink of water. The conversation began about her dream of fresh water which would always be cool and never run out. Gradually, the conversation turned to Christ himself who could quench her spiritual thirst.

Christ chose a place where it was possible to set up communication, and then invite someone to dialogue on a point that interested her. From a discussion of water, he helped this woman grow in vision and life. From that moment onward, her life was changed.

Thus God moved toward people as a person in Jesus Christ. His approach was not with a book or a system, but with flesh and blood. It was the humanity of Christ that enabled him to speak the language of relationship and to be compassionate when someone was in agony, to be patient when someone was slow and dull, to be joyful when someone had happiness to share, to be angry when someone deliberately closed his heart. His complete identity with us (even now) as a human being makes it possible for us to see where and how God fits into our lives. Christ was and is in dialogue with us, for, as Hebrews 13:28 says: "Jesus Christ is the same yesterday, today and forever."

To be christians, we too must be in dialogue. We must respond to the word of God, Jesus Christ. But we cannot be in dialogue with God, our Father, unless we are in dialogue with all men, our brothers. Our openness to our brothers is the measure of our openness to God.

When we open ourselves to a life of dialogue, our person will be enriched. The invitation to be with others makes it possible to be liberated and redeemed from ourselves. Through others we grow from individual to person. Dialogue is mutually creative of the partners of dialogue. In dialogue we awaken within us creative values that direct us to the freedom of self-acceptance.

Also, in dialogue, we share another's freedom; we share in the very act by which that freedom establishes itself. We embark on self-creation. We are nothing until we are tamed; not being tamed makes us unique in the world. We are special to someone—to another person and the Person.

We not only become creators, but also redeemers. In deciding to become dialogical persons, we redeem ourselves from selfishness. We move from the laws of the jungle, which inevitably results from self-centeredness, and we move to a universal vision and concern. By tearing down the screen of isolation around us, we tear it down for others. Therefore, in redeeming ourselves, we redeem others. We give them a community orientation.

The yeast that leavens the dough, the mustard seed that harbors the birds, the few dimes that beget a fortune, the rejected stone that becomes the cornerstone, all are the product of a christian who understands the message and imitates the life of Christ. They all add up to one thing: the establishment of the kingdom of God in this world.

# DISCUSSION QUESTIONS

1. How does dialogue compare with a contract? How does it differ?

2. Why is privacy important for dialogue? Is friendship possible without it? Explain.

3. What makes friendships sour when our energies are spent on discussing the relationship?

4. Explain how we are liberated from ourselves through dialogue. Does dialogue also put us into a state of self-creation?

# THE PRACTICE OF DIALOGUE

To create dialogue and to build community, we, too, have to be interested in others.

The point of contact may be a discussion group on any topic that would interest others, for example, art, war, the lyrics of a current song, novels. If the chosen topic provides an opportunity to look at life, then the discussion will blossom out, include more people and involve them deeply. Such a discussion can become truly dialogical, for it can lead to the ultimate questions of life. It can allow people to share their basic worries and anxieties, joys and dreams.

Discussion groups like these are completely people oriented. The person introducing himself into the situation does not feel forced into a mold or a structure, because he himself makes the structure. The only setting of the discussion is people coming together to interact on a topic that interests them.

Another way to help dialogue is through the use of film. A good movie is like a parable. The film makes use of striking images and is richly symbolic. It challenges the viewer to think and to imagine. The film communicates through the association of ideas. And the primary way it communicates these ideas is not through the script but through its images. The only requirement is that one respond to the film critically, discriminatingly and discerningly.

The movie gives the viewers a common, vicarious experience. By identifying with the characters, they go through an experience that can bring to the surface their own questions. In raising these questions, the group can relate to them together and search for authentic answers, not in a monological or dogmatic way, but together.

Movies can give the viewers an experience of loneliness, suffering, confusion, sadness, sin, joy, love, salvation and redemption, not as abstract topics, but as they are born of life. Because the experience is one common to all the viewers, the film can provide an exciting basis for fruitful dialogue.

An avenue which is particularly useful for dialogue is the knowledge and use of group dynamics. Adolescent and adult groups like to discuss and share their ideas with others. A trained leader can be the catalyst for the group process; he crystalizes the group's thoughts. The discussion itself should be free-ranging and uninhibited, but not without direction.

The leader of the group gives direction for discussion. He points out the ideas that may have been forgotten, but which deserve special attention. He will point out the facts that support an argument or invalidate it. His task is to listen and to engage everyone in the group. He sets the mood. His is the role of a resource person who does not lord it over the other participants. These are just some of the functions the leader performs.

There are three basic group techniques which do not require special training: Phillips' 66, role-playing and brainstorm-

ing. Phillips' 66, named after its origina-
tor, breaks the larger group into smaller
groups of six people each, who discuss a
topic for only six minutes. Each group has
a discussion secretary. When the topic for
discussion is presented, the leader in each
group asks each individual to give his ideas
in one minute.

After six minutes, the secretary has an
extra minute or so to summarize the
group's conclusions. As he does so, the
members of the group can continue their
discussion. Then each secretary presents
his summary to the larger group. The discussion, then, can be opened to the whole
group, or there can be a debate between
two or more groups that have taken opposite sides. Or even a new topic might be
presented for discussion. There are various
way of continuing the discussion.

One great advantage of the Phillips' 66
method is that it gives everyone a chance
to talk. Even a shy person will be willing to
participate in front of only a few others.
He is less afraid of making a fool of himself before a small group than before a
large one.

Role-playing is another technique for group dynamics. It can be very effective in aiding dialogue. In role-playing, the participants make believe and act out various situations or problems. They participate, in effect, in a spontaneous short skit. The leader presents to the group a plausible situation and then asks volunteers to play out the roles.

The advantages of role-playing are two-fold; it helps the members of the group to observe and correct mistakes in human relations, and it gives them the opportunity to have an emotional as well as an intellectual experience.

The third basic group technique is brainstorming. Everyone is invited to contribute one idea on a topic regardless of the idea's apparent value or nonvalue. Speed is of the essence. The purpose is to get as many ideas as possible so that the group will have grist for more specific and concentrated discussion. The later discussion will eliminate, sift and combine until the most fruitful ideas come to the fore.

The advantage of brainstorming is that it is fast-moving and exciting. Also, it usually manages to release the inhibitions of the participants. When they hear strange-sounding and irrelevant ideas proposed, they gain courage to voice their own.

Another technique for dialogue is the basic group encounter, or sensitivity sessions. Because this is such a powerful instrument, it can be more than a technique for dialogue and can sensitize one to the *life* of dialogue.

Basic group encounter is not the same as group discussions or group therapy. Group discussion is for the purpose of sifting ideas, whereas the basic group encounter deals directly with the personal element. Group therapy, on the other hand, is for the person who already hurts with problems and is in the need of help. Encounter groups are for those who are functioning normally but want to improve their capacity for life and for good relationships.

Basic encounter experiences have been held in various settings for a wide range of individuals from presidents of large corporations to high school drop-outs. These encounters may last for as much as three or four weeks or for as little as two

and one-half days. On a weekend encounter, the pace is gruelling. The participants discuss almost incessantly and take
only a few hours out for meals and sleep.
The number of participants usually varies
from eight to eighteen. The sessions themselves are loosely structured, with a com-
petent leader who facilitates the interaction among the members.

At first the discussions are polite and
stilted since the members are usually
strangers to one another. Gradually, in
the atmosphere of much freedom and little
structure, the individual will begin to relate more on the level of feeling than intellect. In so doing, he will come to understand himself and his relationships more
accurately. The ultimate result is trust and
cohesion in the group.

The result of encounter groups are truly
amazing. Such sessions can bring people
closer together in a shorter time than was
ever thought possible. The intimacy is
similar to that experience of people who
have undergone a crisis together.

And the results are long-lasting. They
carry over beyond the group experience it-

self into daily life. In a group process like this, people learn to become more spontaneous, more closely related to their feelings, more open to experience and more intimate. After the encounter they carry these qualities with them into their own environments.

These are some of the techniques that can be used as avenues to dialogue and building blocks for the community. Not everyone of them is practical for every situation but each one has something to offer to the fulfillment of the human person. One of the techniques could be used in your own city block, in your club, in your parish, or with your fellow-workers. Each one humanizes the person and helps him to relate better with his fellowman, and, therefore, is a very valid technique for contemporary christianity.

# ❋ ❋

# SUGGESTED
# READINGS

Buber, Martin. *I and Thou*. New York: Charles Scribner's Sons, 1958.

——————. *Between Man and Man*. New York: Macmillan, 1965.

Day, Albert E. *Dialogue and Destiny*. New York: Harper Brothers, 1961.

de Chardin, Pierre Teilhard. *The Phenomenon of Man*. New York: Harper & Row, 1959.

de Saint-Exupery, Antoine. *The Little Prince*. New York: Harcourt, Brace and World, 1943.

Frankl, Viktor E. *Man's Search for Meaning*. New York: Washington Square Press, 1963.

Howe, Reuel L. *Man's Need and God's Action*. New York: Seabury Press, 1953.

——————. *The Miracle of Dialogue*. New York: Seabury Press, 1963.

Tournier, Paul. *The Meaning of Persons.* New York: Harper & Row, 1957.

Wicker, Brian. *Culture and Theology.* London: Sheed & Ward, 1966.

# MULTI-MEDIA

ALL KINDS OF PEOPLE
*13 min. 6 mm. Color. Produced by Precedent Films, Inc., 1965. For sale from Sterling Educational Films, 309 West Jackson Boulevard, Chicago, Illinois 60606. May also be rented from some film libraries.*

The world is made up of many different people who live in differing ways. Can they not live in peace? By contrasting war with culture, this film shows the futility of modern weaponry and the necessity of a world law for peace. The film emphasizes the totality of mankind.

THE CITY AS MAN'S HOME
*28 min. 16 mm. b&w. Produced by the National Film Board of Canada (part V of the Lewis Mumford "On the City" series), 1963. Available from Mass Media Ministries, 2116 North Charles Street, Baltimore, Maryland 21218. Rental: $8.00.*

This documentary treats the rise of faceless, depersonalized housing and its effects upon human psychology. It contrasts the modern depersonalization of society with that community which man naturally longs for and needs.

### MOMENT TO ACT

*29 min. 16 mm. b&w. Produced by the Broadcasting and Film Commission, NCC, 1962. National Council of Churches, 475 Riverside Drive, New York, New York 10027. May also be rented from many denominational libraries.*

A young woman returns to her home after an extended stay in a mental institution. She is met with misunderstanding and misguided attempts on the part of her mother and church to accept her back into the community. The audience is left with the feeling that many professing christians may have limited senses of christian responsibilities.

### NEIGHBORS

*9 min. 16 mm. Color. Produced by the National Film Board of Canada, 1952. Available from the International Film Bureau, 332 South Michigan Avenue, Chicago, Illinois 60604. Also, Contemporary Films, Inc., 828 Custer Avenue, Evanston, Illinois.*

A flower springs up on the property line between two neighbors. As greed gets the better of them, each claims it as his own.

Their covetousness results in the destruction of everything, including themselves.

### NEIGHBORS NEED NEIGHBORS

*One set of thirty photos, 17½″ x 17½″. b&w. Produced by the Executive Council of the Episcopal Church. Available from Seabury Bookstores, 815 Second Avenue, New York, New York 10017. Sale: $5.00.*

The need to involve oneself in all facets of community to be aware of what can be done to meet the needs of others is strongly highlighted in these photos.

### POWER AMONG MEN

*44 min. 16 mm. Color and b&w. Produced by United Nations, 1959. Available from De Rochemont Film Library, 267 West 25th Street, New York, New York 10001. Also available from many film libraries.*

This is a dramatic and moving portrait, depicting man's potential to use power to build or destroy. Without preaching, the film's impact forces the viewer to consider which way man will go.

### WHY AM I AFRAID TO LOVE?

*Five 7″ tapes of nine lectures by John Powell, S.J. Produced by Argus Communications. Available for sale from the producer, 3505 North Ashland Avenue, Chicago, Illinois 60657. 3¾ ips, $14.50; 1⅞ ips, $10.90. Also for rent from some religious tape libraries.*

In a terse, hard-hitting, thought-provoking manner, Father Powell asks why we have made God to our image and likeness, why we try to buy him off, why we roll gifts his way to buy him off. Is this love? The lecturer goes on to examine the capacity and yearning for love in each of us and the fear which prohibits our loving.